White in the Flag

by Mobeen Ansari

White in the Flag by Mobeen Ansari
First published in Pakistan in 2017 by Markings Publishing
Second edition published in Pakistan in 2022 by Markings Publishing

Photographer
Mobeen Ansari

Book Layout & Design by
Samia Fatima at Markings

Text Editing by
Raisa Vayani at Markings

ISBN: 978-969-9251-93-1

MARKINGS
PUBLISHING
info@markings.com.pk
www.markings.com.pk

To my mother, to whom I owe
more than words can express

Introduction

More than 35 years ago, before I was born, my father was diagnosed with abdominal tuberculosis, which had reached a critical stage. During the surgery he lost so much blood that he urgently needed two bags of blood. Not only that, but precisely the exact same blood type as well. Two of his friends stepped up and donated their blood. One of them was his best friend, a Christian, Ronald Umar Khitab.

This saved my father's life. And I am here now! And so I began the journey towards making this book.

An attack of meningitis at a very early age impacted my hearing, eyesight, and balance. These challenges shaped my life and its directions of not being 'normal', 'acceptable', and being a part of the comfortable majority of 'normal' people. I would like to express my deepest gratitude to all the people who have assisted me, especially my parents, mainly the dedication of my mother.

The definition of a new 'normal' is not based on race, religion, politics, money, or physical attributes. It is based on the basic truths of everyone being equal.

My first book (*Dharkan –The Heartbeat of a Nation*) was a result of that. It was an effort to have people see the essential goodness in my country and the people who have made Pakistan.

This book, '*White in the Flag*', is a continuation of that very journey.

It has taken me into a space of personal discovery – where I have attended Christmas parties at my friends' houses, to meeting and loving the delightfully vast and colorful range of people who are embedded in the warp and weave of the fabric of this country.

As I started my quest I did not realize the diversity, depth and vibrancy of the multitude of religions, cultures, and subcultures that make up the fabric of Pakistan. With every step I would discover aspects of the lives of the people who reside in my country, which would leave me even more determined to explore it further.

This journey has enabled me to search my own self as I viewed the human condition. It has been an amazing journey which has only just begun, but I still feel that I have 'miles to go before I sleep'.

I am very fortunate to have been able to put this book together. I'm fortunate because of how much it has enriched me and how much I have seen and learnt in the process.

Whether it was witnessing colors of Holi at many mandirs in Tharparkar, or listening to hymns at the Sunday mass at Saint Anthony's church in Lahore, to joining in on the festivities of Chowmos - a Kalash festival - I have been able to see, capture and celebrate diversity.

I must admit that I could never do justice to this vast and vital subject. I could not cover the diversity and depth of the different communities as much as I would have liked to.

White in the Flag took me across the parched deserts in Sindh, to the pristine mountains of the North, to the many temples and places of worship in every nook and cranny of urban cities. It gave me the opportunity to interact with people of all faiths, which has been a truly fascinating and an eye-opening experience. By interacting with the communities (I prefer not to call them minorities), I have learnt far more about my country and religion than I have from any other experience.
It has been a very exciting, sobering and educating adventure.

This book and its title…

The green in the Pakistan flag represents Islam, the majority religion; and the white stripe represents religious minorities and minority religions. The crescent and star symbolize progress and light.

The flag symbolizes Pakistan's commitment to Islam and the rights of religious minorities.

It stems from the clear instructions of the Prophet Mohammad (PBUH),

"Beware! Whoever is cruel and hard on a non-Muslim minority, or curtails their rights, or burdens them with more than they can bear, or takes anything from them against their free will; I (Prophet Muhammad) will complain against the person on the Day of Judgment." (Abu Dawud)

And this determined saying of Mohammad Ali Jinnah, who said:

"You are free; you are free to go to your temples, you are free to go to your mosques or to any other place of worship in this State of Pakistan. You may belong to any religion or caste or creed that has nothing to do with the business of the State". In the same speech he said, "We are starting in the days where there is no discrimination, no distinction between one community and another, no discrimination between one caste or creed and another. We are starting with this fundamental principle: that we are all citizens, and equal citizens, of one State."
Along the way, some of us have forgotten these precepts and promises.

Hence the title of this book.

A note on the second edition

In the five years that followed the publication of *White in the Flag's* first edition in 2017, the book's journey continued. I was privileged to witness and photograph many more celebrations and places of worship. This time, I was fortunate to document some aspects of Buddhism in Pakistan, which is home to many historical and sacred Buddhist sites. A few historical events took place during this time as well, such as the opening of Kartarpur corridor in November of 2019, which brought together Sikhs (and people of other faiths) from around the world to Guru Nanak's final resting place.

This edition comprises over 30 new photographs. I feel that this book's story and my experiences have evolved parallel to one another and reflects a better understanding of the tapestry of faiths in Pakistan. I have tried to do justice to the richness of this subject matter and I hope that you enjoy this journey as much as I have by sharing this with you.

\- Mobeen Ansari

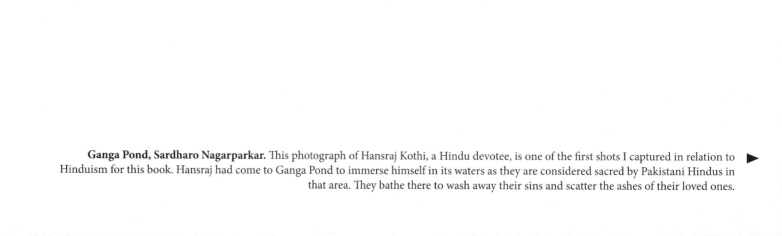

Ganga Pond, Sardharo Nagarparkar. This photograph of Hansraj Kothi, a Hindu devotee, is one of the first shots I captured in relation to Hinduism for this book. Hansraj had come to Ganga Pond to immerse himself in its waters as they are considered sacred by Pakistani Hindus in that area. They bathe there to wash away their sins and scatter the ashes of their loved ones.

Kalash Valley. Kalash children gather to make a fire in a practice known as Sarazari on the eve of Chowmos. The Kalash have a festival for every ▲
season and Chowmos is the winter festival. It lasts for 14 days and is the most significant of these festivals.

Nankana Sahib. 'Panj pyaray', or the beloved five, lead the procession on the second day of Janam Din Baba Guru Nanak Dev ▶
ji, or the birthday of the founder of Sikhism, Guru Nanak. It is held at the Gurdwara Janam Asthaan, the birthplace of Guru
Nanak. Sikh pilgrims come from all over the world for this celebration.

▲ **Bamboret, Kalash Valley.** Kalashi women wish each other well at one of the dances during Joshi, the Kalash Festival of Spring

◀ **Swaminarain Mandir, Karachi.** I came across these boys having fun while photographing my first ever Holi festival.

▲ **Baha'I Hall Karachi.** Celebrations for the festival of Eid Ridván. It is a 12-day Baha'i festival that celebrates the declaration by their founder Bahá'u'lláh of his being a Manifestation of God.

◄ **Christ Church, Rawalpindi.** Members of the choir sing during the Christmas service. I visited this Presbyterian Church many times with my family during my childhood to celebrate Christmas and Easter with our Christian neighbours.

Nankana Sahib. Celebrations underway at Gurdwara Janam Asthan, for the birthday of Guru Nanak. ▲

All Saints Church, Peshawar. A quiet moment at the altar in the Protestant church in Peshawar. ▶

Gurdwara Janam Asthan, Nankana Sahib. Sikh devotees listening quietly to Shabad Kirtan being performed. The text from the Guru Granth Sahib is the most sacred text in Sikhism. Shabad Kirtan is the musical reciting of this text. ▲

Christ Church, Rawalpindi. A crowded church for the Easter Sunday service. ▶

Karachi. The 1600 year old Panjmuki Maharaj ▶
Hanoman Mandir in Karachi.

◀ **Cathedral Church of the Resurrection, Lahore.**
This photograph was captured moments after Sunday
mass. The cathedral is one of the most historic and
beautiful churches in Pakistan and is the principal
church of the Roman Catholic Archdiocese of
Lahore.

Takht-i-Bahi Buddhist Monastery, Mardan. ▶
A closeup of the monastery. The buildings are
constructed of stone with a lime and mud mortar.

◀ **Takht-i-Bahi Buddhist Monastery, Mardan.** A
view of the monastery that dates back to 1st-7th
century AD and is considered one of the most
important relics of Buddhism. Interestingly it was
also said to be a Zoroastrian complex in its first
construction period.

Dosabhai Meherwanji Wadia Dar-e-Meher Pakistan Chowk, Karachi. An Agyari (Zoroastrian fire temple) in Pakistan Chowk. Its origins can be dated back to 28th May 1869.

Baha'I Hall, Islamabad. A nine-pointed star on the roof of the Baha'i hall in the Baha'i centre, Islamabad. The nine points represent the 9 major religions of the world. They symbolize a Baha'i teaching that the source of all religions is One. The number 9 also has two other meanings in the Baha'i teaching. Firstly it represents the number of perfection, it being the highest single number and secondly it is the numerical value of the word 'Baha'.

▲ **(All Indian Israelite League) Karachi:** This is one of the first known photos of Jews in Karachi, who were and are also known as the Bani/Bene Israel Tribe, which was also the name of Jews living in the subcontinent in India and Pakistan. The photograph was taken at the first meeting of the 'All Indian Israeilite League' in December 1918. Their President was one Abraham Reuben, who at that meeting was asked to represent the 650 Jews in Sind in relation to the Zionist movement. The Karachi community asked him to visit the Holy Land in Israel to report on the possibility of immigrating there. The League had a journal called Israelite (where this photo first appeared) and they were more educated and supportive of Indian nationalism and less parochial than the Bene Israel conference which was set up at the same time and who opposed them and focused on more narrow Bene Israel interests. (Information courtesy Dr. Shalva Weil)

◀ **Rawalpindi.** There used to be a considerable population of Jews in Pakistan and the Star of David can be found engraved on many older buildings. I found this on a building which looked like it had been an old synagogue. The last known synagogue was in Karachi, so it is unclear if this building was also one, although the symbol does appear more than once on it.

◀ **Karachi.** This Bene Israel (or Jews of the subcontinent) family photo of the Nowgaokar family was taken in Karachi in 1924. The man standing is the late Ephraim Joseph Nowgaokar (1893-1938) and the woman sitting is his wife Ya'akobeth Abraham Nowgaokar. It also shows their children Moses, Jerusha, Enoch, Dina & Ruth. Whilst speaking with Eliaz Reuben-Dandekar, who generously provided this photo for the book, I came to realise that the very same Ephraim in this photograph is actually buried in the Jewish cemetery in Karachi which is shown later in this book. Photo courtesy: Eliaz Reuben-Dandeker and late Gershon Ephraim Nowgaokar of Karachi.

Magen Shalom Synagogue, Karachi. ▶
The Bar-Mitzvah of Moses Ephraim
Nowgaokar (1917-1988) standing on far
left, in the Magen Shalom Synagogue in
Karachi. This synagogue, built in 1893
and completed on the 21st May of that
year, was sadly demolished on 17th July
1988. With him are his sister Jerusha
(1918-1980) and brother Enoch (1920-
1969). Photo courtesy: Eliaz Reuben-
Dandeker, originally provided by his
late grandmother Mrs. Anni (Hannah)
Nowgaokar the wife of Moses.

▲ **Takht-i-Bahi Buddhist Monastery, Mardan.** A view of the Takht-i-Bahi monastery nestled in the mountains. This monastic complex has been through many different eras spanning seven centuries. It's position on top of high hills gave it some protection from the many invasions that spanned the centuries, leaving it in a well preserved state.

◀ **Kargah Buddha carving on the outskirts of Gilgit.** It is a 7th century carved image of a standing Buddha measuring up to 50 feet and the carving is done in an unusual Baltistan style. Buddhism arrived in this region in the 7th century.

Gurdwara Kartarpur Sahib. Sikh pilgrims at the re-opening of the newly renovated Gurdwara Kartarpur Sahib in 2019, as they listen to speeches by politicians from India and Pakistan. This occasion was also historic as it saw the opening of the Kartarpur corridor, a visa free corridor between Pakistan and India opened by the Government of Pakistan so that Sikh pilgrims from around the world could visit one of the most important sites of Sikhism more easily when travelling from India. It links this Gurdwara in Pakistan with Gurdwara Dera Baba Nanak just over the border in India.

Gurdwara Kartarpur Sahib. Another scene at Gurdwara Katarpur Sahib on the occasion of the opening of the Kartarpur corridor. This Gurdwara is one of the holiest sites in Sikhism as Guru Nanak , the founder of Sikhism, established his first commune here and it is also where he died.

▲ **A beautifully lit Gurdwara Kartarpur Sahib at night.** Guru Nanak built this gurdwara on the right bank of the Ravi river. But over the years following his death the course of the river changed and swept away some of the mausoleums that had been built on the site. Guru Nanak also had Muslim followers and they ensured the preservation of the temple over the years until its reopening in 2019.

◄ **Gurdwara Punja Sahib.** Nightfall over Gurdwara Punja Sahib, on the night of Baisakhi (harvest) festival. This Gurdwara is largely famous for the boulder that contains the handprint of Guru Nanak, which happened as a result of him stopping it with his hand, after it was rolled down by Saint Wali Kandhari.

Kali Mata Mandir, Umerkot, Tharparkar. A man lighting small lamps or diyas on the eve of the Hindu festival of Diwali. ▲

Saint Joseph's Cathedral, Rawalpindi. Midnight Easter vigil at the cathedral. ▶

▲ **Holi Jo Daro, Mithi.** The burning of the Holika fire symbolising the triumph of good over evil, on the eve of Holi.

◀ **Saint Joseph's Cathedral, Rawalpindi.** Devotees at the midnight Easter mass.

Kalash Valley. The Kalasha community gather to make a big fire on the second day of Chowmos. The boys help the girls to make as big a smoke as possible so that the girls can get more blessings. ▲

Lahore. Candlelight after midnight mass on Christmas Eve at Saint Anthony's Catholic Church, Lahore. ▶

▲ **Gurdwara Punja Sahib.** Nagar Kirtan at Baisakhi festival at Gurdwara Punja Sahib. Baisakhi is celebrated to mark the beginning of a new harvest season.

◄ **Badin Sindh.** Celebrating the Hindu Thudhri festival at a Mandir in Badin. Thudhri (which means cold in the Sindhi language) is dedicated to the folk deity Shitala Devi, who is believed to cure poxes, sores, ghouls and diseases. It is Sindh specific (as the statue of Shitala was discovered in Moen Jo Daro when it was excavated) so it is celebrated by Sindhi Hindus worldwide.

Kalash Valley. Naseera Kalash, a nurse and polio worker who has worked at Bamboret hospital in Kalash for many years. ▲

Ramboor Valley, Kalash. Erica Kalash and her child. ▶

▲ **Gurdwara Kartarpur Sahib.** A Sikh pilgrim at the Gurdwara.

◀ **Badin, Sindh.** Rani and her child prepare to leave for the Thudhri festival. Rani and the residents of her village are some of the most beautiful people I have photographed.

▲ **Karachi.** Rashna Gazder is a famous Parsi piano teacher and concert pianist based in Karachi. She has been playing and teaching for 27 years and has taught generations of piano players.

◀ **Umerkot, Tharparkar.** Carrying home the water pitchers.

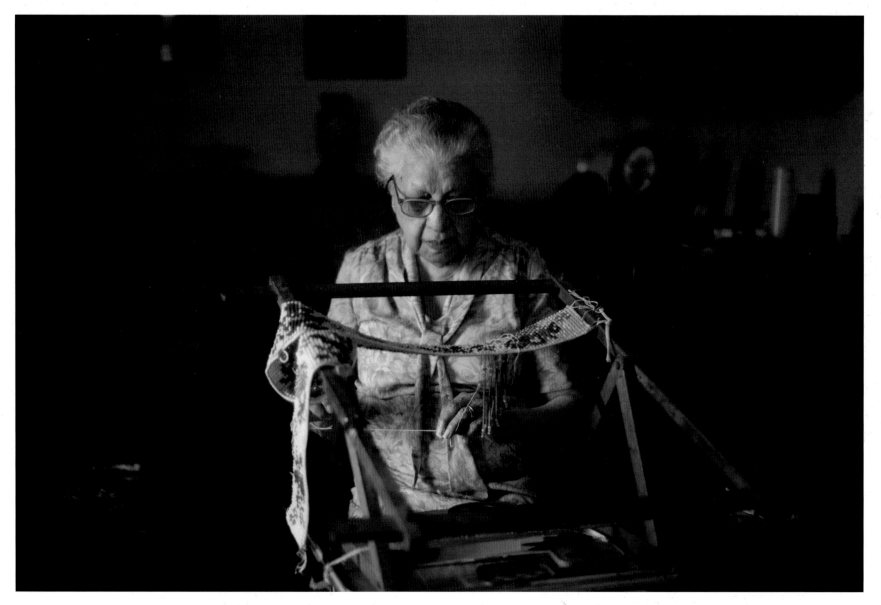

Karachi. Rashidbano Virjee is a Parsi lady who makes Torans, a decorative piece to put on doorways for prosperity and good luck. She has been making them for 55 years and is the last of her family to do so. It is now a dying art since very few people have the motivation or urge to learn this. ▲

Kalash Valley. Sichin Bibi Kalash (late) was a herbal doctor and one of the most famous faces in Kalash valley. I met her for the first time on my very first trip to Kalash years ago. Before I went, I looked up photos of her online as she has been photographed many times by photographers from all over the world. I printed them out and took them with me to Kalash, as I knew this would be the best way to find her. The villagers there gladly took me to her. ▶

Karachi. Madavsaro is a Zoroastrian/Parsi pre wedding ceremony, which depicts bonding and prosperity. The ritual of the elements used in the ceremony serves as a reminder that life is made up of all factors- the good, the bad, the sweet and the bitter. ▲

Karachi Parsi Institute, Karachi. The Navjote ceremony of Dea Umrigar. It is a ritual in which an individual is inducted into the Zoroastrian religion and begins to wear the Sudreh (undergarment) and the Kushti (a sacred girdle), which is being tied around Dea in this picture by the high priest Berjise Bhada. ▶

▲ **Nankana Sahib.** A Sikh student looks directly at the camera during class.

◄ **Baha'I Centre Islamabad.** A student interacting with her teacher in a Children's Class, one of the educational initiatives of the Baha'i. Children are the future of this world, and the Baha'i community aims to give them spiritual nourishment especially in a world and time where the joy and innocence of childhood can be easily overwhelming.

Swaminarain Mandir, Karachi. Girls pose for a photo during the festival of Holi. ▲

Bamboret, Kalash. Young Kalashi girls during Sarazari at the Chowmos festival. ▶

Kalash Valley. Bibi Kai Kalash is a hotel owner and another famous face in Kalash valley. I have often returned to photograph her and on my last visit I became her adopted grandson. ▶

◀ **Bamboret, Kalash.** Noorjahan Kalash observing the dance during the Joshi festival of Spring.

▲ **Gurdwara Janam Asthaan, Nankana Sahib.** Sikh pilgrims pose for a photo during Guru Nanak's birthday celebrations.

◄ **Gurdwara Bhai Joga Singh, Peshawar.** A Sikh devotee in prayer at the Gurdwara in Peshawar, where there is a considerable Sikh population in Khyber Pakhtunkhwa province. The Gurdwara was founded by Hari Singh Nalwa, Maharaja Ranjit Singh's general, when Peshawar was part of the Sikh Kingdom. It is named in honour of Bhai Joga Singh, a young Gursikh.

Badin, Sindh. Sumi, a local of Badin. ▲

Parsi General Hospital, Karachi. Gulbano Bamji (right), a social worker and a member on the board of the Parsi General Hospital with a patient (Bomi Shekhdar). ▶
She hails from Quetta, which also has a small population of Parsis living there. On the day I met Gulbano, I had been with a Parsi friend who had taken me to many of the places I needed to photograph, like the Karachi Parsi Institute, the two Agyaris and more. At lunchtime he took me to the hospital, where a lunch had been prepared. On that table sat two Parsis (one of them being Gulbano), a Hindu, a Christian, and myself, a Muslim. It was a beautiful experience having lunch with people from different faiths and backgrounds. It was a defining moment for the rest of my book.

Parsi General Hospital, Karachi. The KB Nusserwanjee R. Mehta infirmary, built in October 1965. The Parsi General Hospital is one ▲ of the many contributions of the community to the city of Karachi. It runs on donations from members of the community.

Heerjibhoy J. Behrana Parsi Dar-e Meher, Saddar Agyari Karachi. Ervad Jehangirjee Noshirwan Sidhwa, Head Priest of Saddar ▶ Agyari in Karachi (left) and the late Ervad Jal Dinshawjee Pohwala (right). Ervad Jal used to assist the head priest with all prayers.

▲ **Christ Church Rawalpindi.** Reverend Emmanuel Lorrain, Vicar of Saint Thomas Church Islamabad, consecrating the Holy Communion on Christmas Day.

◀ **Cathedral Church of the Resurrection, Lahore.** A group of nuns pose for a photo at the cathedral.

▲ **Karachi.** The Katrak swimming bath is the oldest building on the premises of the Karachi Parsi Institute. It was built in 1905.

◀ **Karachi.** Parsi men playing cards at the Karachi Parsi Institute, where they get together every evening.

Bamboret, Kalash valley. A dance on the last day of the Joshi festival. During this festival, which marks the arrival of spring, the community picks leaves from nearby trees and dance.

◀ **Nankana Sahib** A Sikh family goes shopping after the first day of Guru Nanak's birthday celebrations.

Lahore. Christmas Eve mass at Saint Joseph's Church. This was my first midnight mass experience. ▲

Gurdwara Janam Asthaan, Nankana Sahib. A Sikh procession leading a bus carrying Granth Sahib on the second day of Guru Nanak's birthday celebrations. Granth Sahib is the religious scripture of Sikhism. In fact it is more than just that – it is regarded and respected by Sikhs as their living Guru, as it contains the actual words spoken by the founders of Sikhism. ▶

▲ **Umerkot, Sindh.** A devotee at Kali Mata mandir.

◀ **Umerkot, Sindh.** Children playing with firecrackers on Diwali.

Christ Church, Rawalpindi. Listening to the sermon during the Christmas Day service. ▲

Karachi. Eid e Ridván inside Baha'i Hall. ▶

▲ **Islamabad.** Worship at a humble home church in a Christian neighborhood in Islamabad. It was interesting to see eastern instruments being used especially the harmonium.

◀ **Islamabad.** Junior Youth Spiritual Empowerment at the Baha'i Centre. Adolescents go through physical and emotional changes. This period of life is very sensitive, as increased awareness and interest can shape the rest of their lives. At the same time, it also attracts doubts, discomfort and other negative emotions. The Baha'i feel directing these adolescents' new abilities towards selfless service to humanity is therefore needed at this age.

Karachi. A Parsi wedding, of Sarah and Sharoy. ►

◄ **Saint Christopher Church, Karachi.** Wedding of one of the couples at a mass wedding ceremony

▲ **Kalash Valley.** Celebrating Joshi. Here, a Kalashi is wearing the national flag on their head as part of the celebrations.

◀ **Bahá'i Nowruz celebrations at the Bahá'i Centre in Islamabad.** The Bahá'i new year starts on the 21st March and a gathering is always held on that day to celebrate the new year; many friends from all walks of life are invited to celebrate the new spring together.

Mithi, Interior Sindh. Holi celebrations outside Krishna Mandir. ▲

Karachi. The Nauroz eve dance at the Karachi Parsi Institute. The community gathers here ▶
in large numbers and celebrates until the wee hours of the morning.

▲ **Karachi.** A Nauroz table by Mrs Roshan Mehri. Everyone celebrating Nauroz sets up a table called Haft-Seen. It's an arrangement of seven symbolic items all starting with the letter Seen (S). It includes *Sabzeh* which consists of wheat, barley, mung bean or lentil sprouts growing in a dish to symbolize rebirth; *Samanu*, a sweet pudding made from wheat germ to symbolize affluence; *Senjed*, a dried Persian olive to symbolize love; *Seer* meaning garlic, to symbolize medicine and health; *Seeb* or apple to symbolize beauty; *Somāq*, sumac fruit to symbolize the colours of sunrise and *Serkeh,* vinegar to symbolize old-age and patience. The photo of the Prophet Zoroaster is also displayed.

◀ **Karachi.** A traditional Nauroz Parsi welcome. A few drops of rose water are poured onto the palms of guests so that their next year may pass by in sweet fragrance. They also hold a mirror up to the guest so that they may see their own reflection and thus a clear and bright future for themselves. Here, the host Mrs. Roshan Mehri holds a mirror and rose water for Natasha Mavalwalla.

Ramboor, Kalash valley. A woman brewing red wine. In the Kalash faith, wine is considered to be ▲
purifying and is an important part of the culture. It is used in their rituals as well as for recreational use.

Kalash Valley. A hotelier, Zafar Khan Kalash, drinking a glass of red wine. ▶

▲ **Nankana Sahib.** Water being served at Gurdwara Janam Asthaan. The people serving the water are performing sewa or voluntary work for others.

◀ **Bamboret Valley, Kalash.** A girl stands next to the roof of her family home. It was the day before the beginning of Joshi and I had just arrived in the valley for the celebrations. I came across this girl standing as she is, and captured her as she looked at me.

▲ **Nankana Sahib.** Langar at Gurdwara Janam Asthaan on the first day of Guru Nanak's birthday celebrations. Langar is a term used in Sikhism to signify a common kitchen/canteen where everyone is fed free of charge – regardless of background, faith, caste or creed. All the food served is vegetarian so that no religious group is offended.

◄ **A Gahambar in Karachi.** It is a month of feasting in the Parsi calendar, where the community gets together to eat and share food communally, in a demonstration of beliefs, principles and values in action and an expression of piety in thought, word and deed.

Nankana Sahib. Sikh youth washing utensils after Langar. ▲

Nankana Sahib. Two Sikh friends share a light moment outside a Gurdwara. ▶

Karachi. A member of the congregation ▶ speaking on Eid e Ridván. There are no clergy in the Baha'I faith so anyone, including children, can address the congregation. Children often recite poetry at these celebrations.

◀ **Badin, Sindh.** Worshippers gathered for pooja at a mandir in Badin during the Thudhri festival.

▲ **Islamabad.** Outside the Seventh Day Adventist Church in a Christian neighborhood in Islamabad.

◀ **Karachi.** A devotee in a trance at Saint Andrew's Presbyterian Church.

Islamabad. A Baha'I lady reads from her book of prayers.

Bamboret. Johar Baig (late) was also known by the title 'Khaosaggao Bandawow' which means 'the man who announces festivals'. He conducted all the rituals relating to the Kalash religion, and announced the coming of all festivals for more than 40 years - particularly in Bamboret valley in Kalash. I remember very clearly the first time I saw him. He was dancing at the Joshi festival and swinging his axe around as part of a ritual. I tracked him down again a few years later in his home, where this photo was taken.

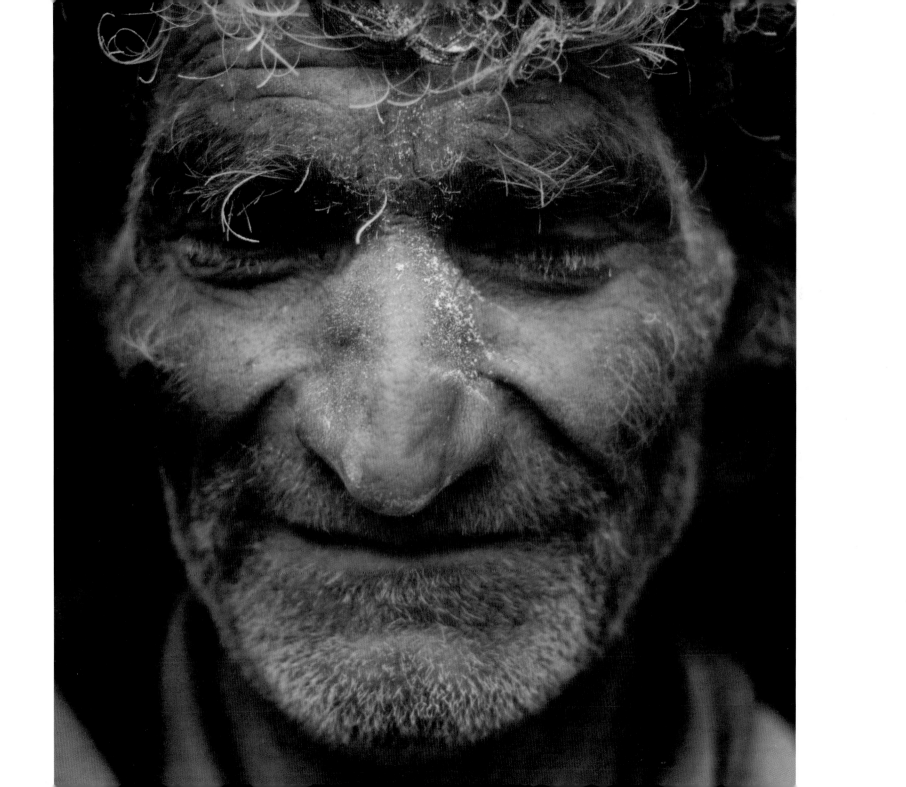

▲ **Karachi.** A lady offering pooja at Panjmukhi Maharaj Hanoman Mandir.

◀ **Rawalpindi.** A man deep in prayer during Easter service at Christ Church.

▲ **The Hinglaj Mata Mandir on the Makran coast of Balochistan**. A Hindu temple in a small natural cave. It is dedicated to Hinglaj Mata who is said to be a powerful deity who bestows good to all her devotees. It is an important place of pilgrimage in Pakistan and Hinglaj Yatra is the largest Hindu pilgrimage in the country, in which more than 250,000 people take part every spring.

◄ **Nankana Sahib.** A Sikh pilgrim praying at Gurdwara Janam Asthaan.

◀ **Saint Patrick's Cathedral, Karachi.** A moment of solitude after Sunday service.

Islamabad. Baha'i prayers ▶ at a home in Islamabad. It is common for the community to offer prayers at Baha'i centres or in one another's homes.

Islamabad. Members of the Baha'i community praying. They sit in a circle and take turns to say different ▲
forms of prayers in different languages. Here, they are listening to another's prayers in silence.

Cathedral Church of the Resurrection, Lahore. Sister Angelina deep in prayer. ▶

▲ **Gurdwara Bhai Biba Singh, Peshawar.** Sikh devotees bowing to Granth Sahib at the Gurdwara. This Gurdwara is almost three centuries old. It was established at the time of the 10th Sikh guru, Gobind Singh. It was not in use for six decades, until it was handed to the Sikh community in 2016.

◀ **Saint Dominic's Church, Bahawalpur.** Father Nadeem Joseph walks through the Church, built in 1962.

▲ **Kalash Valley.** A Kalash girl tends to the fire to make more smoke during the ritual of Sarazari. As described in an earlier photograph, the more smoke the girls make the bigger the blessing they receive.

◄ **Nankana Sahib.** A devotee offering a prayer called Ardas, after listening to the Kirtan recitation at Gurdwara Janam Asthan.

Cathedral Church of the Resurrection, Lahore. Sister Angelina in a moment of prayer at the altar. ▲

Karachi. Berjise Bhada, a Parsi priest, tends to the fire while celebrating the Jashan festival of thanksgiving at his home. ▶

Bahawalpur Museum. Detail of a statue of Buddha. Many Buddhist statues and artifacts have been discovered around the country and have ▲ been taken from their original settings for preservation purposes and are now housed in museums across Pakistan.

Mehrabpur, Sindh. Jumman, the leader of a small Buddhist community conducting a ritual. ▶

▲ **Karachi.** An image of Zoroaster hanging above the door of Roshan Mehri's home.

◀ **Karachi.** A prayer table is set up in every Parsi home to honour their ancestors and the prophet Zoroaster.

gloria in excelsis Deo

Saint Joseph's Church, Lahore. A crib depicting the Nativity of Christ.

Sukkur, Sindh. Inside Jhoolay Laal Zinda Pir Mandir.

Katasraj Temples, Chakwal. One ▶ of the seven temples housed in the Katasraj complex.

◀ **Manora Island, Karachi.** The altar inside the historic Varun Dev Mandir. This mandir is devoted to Varuna, the Hindu God of water. One can also see images of Guru Nanak inside. When I visited, restoration work was underway and I found out that the team involved came from all faiths. It was my last photograph for the book and it was a beautiful way to end this journey.

Karachi. A Jewish cemetery inside the Mewa Shah graveyard in Karachi. It was very interesting to see tombstones written ▲ not only in English and Hebrew but in the Marathi script as well.

Mewa Shah graveyard, Karachi. Mehr-dun-Nisa and her family have been gravekeepers of this Jewish cemetery for ▶ centuries. She continues to protect it to this day. The family is not Jewish but this is what they have always done.

◀ **Bamboret, Kalash valley.** An inscription on a pillar inside the Jasthakan, a hall where dead bodies are brought for prayers before burial.

Bamboret, Kalash valley. One of the ▶ open graves in Bamboret. Open graves used to be the standard form of burial for the Kalash, but since more people have started coming to the valley, many now bury their dead under upturned charpoys.

▲ **Avari Colony, Karachi.** The Farvardian. A prayer hall, where prayers are said from time to time to honour the dead.

◄ **Birir, Kalash valley.** A new graveyard in Birir. The overturned charpoys in the photo are the ones the deceased passed away on. Sometimes they are left there, sometimes they are taken back.

Karachi. The Dakhma, or Tower of Silence, is a round structure in which Zoroastrians lay their dead, to be disposed of by the rays of the sun. ▲
This is an ancestral Dakhma, one of the two in Avari Colony.

Swat Valley. The Saidu Sharif Stupa, a sacred Buddhist location on the outskirts of the valley. ▶

▲ **Rawalpindi.** A grave in the Christian graveyard Gora Qabristan. British Royal Army soldiers who fought in the two great wars are also buried here, hence the name 'Gora Qabristan'. It is one of the oldest (over two centuries old) Christian cemeteries in Rawalpindi and is shared by both the Protestant Church of Pakistan and the Catholic Church.

◄ **Karachi.** A grave in the Jewish cemetery in the Mewa Shah graveyard.

◀ **Dusk over Gurdwara Kartarpur Sahib.**

Bahawalpur Museum. A stone ▶
carving titled Mahaprinirvana, or
death of Buddha, which depicts the
body of Buddha lying on his deathbed
surrounded by mourners.

Rawalpindi. The queue for communion during the Christmas service at Christ Church. ▲

Kalash Valley. On the first day of the Joshi festival in Kalash, women with their newborns and young ones go to a goat stable for purification as ▶
it is considered to be a pure place. Newborns are purified with water, while babies are purified with milk and older children are purified with red
wine. When a boy turns seven, he is purified with goat blood.

▲ **Krishna Mandir, Mithi.** A man is raised so he can break the Matki (pitcher) during Holi. It is interesting to note that this is not practiced by Hindus in India. Matki is usually broken on Janamashtmi, which is the birthday of Lord Krishna. It is filled with yoghurt or pure white butter, as Lord Krishna used to love dairy products. He would break the Matkis of his milkmaids when he saw them returning with their pitchers having fetched not milk and honey, but water. Hindus in Pakistan especially in Mithi, have their own unique customs and way of celebrating things.

◀ **Mehrabpur, Sindh.** Jumman leading some of the Buddhist community in Mehrabpur in worship.

Gurdwara Janam Asthaan Nankana Sahib. A volunteer at Guru Nanak's birthday celebrations doing seva by cleaning the Charan Kamal or water pit, through which devotees walk to clean their feet before entering the Gurdwara premises.

Nankana Sahib. Pilgrims walking through the Charan Kamal at Gurdwara Janam Asthaan. The main entrance into the Gurdwara is called the 'Deodi', and the Charan Kamal is always placed underneath.

Gurdwara Punja Sahib, Hasan Abdal. A Sikh devotee swims in the sacred pond of the Gurdwara. ▲

Gurdwara Punja Sahib, Hasan Abdal. Baisakhi festival being held at the Gurdwara. Sikh ▶
pilgrims from around the world attend this festival every year in large numbers.

▲ **Karachi.** In the Zoroastrian calendar there is a day believed to be the birthday of water known as Ava Roj and Ava Mahino in Gujarati and in English Ava day and Ava month. In the picture, a Parsi family prays and throws offerings of respect to the water at a beachfront in Karachi. The offerings consist of coconut, roses and milk.

◄ **Sadh Belo Mandir, Sukkur.** Hindu devotees travel to Sadh Belo Mandir on an island in Sukkur to pay their respects. It is one of the most important places for Hindus in Sindh.

Karachi. On Ava Roj, a Parsi girl ties Kusti around her waist before saying her prayers, as is customary. The kusti or kushti is a hollow cord made from 72 threads of lamb's wool. It is wrapped three times around the waist, over the sudrah. Different meanings are derived from the name ranging from it being an ancient Aryan identifier to a destroyer of evil. The significance of wrapping the kusti three times around the waist is to wrap oneself in the pledge to abide by good thoughts, good words and good deeds. The kusti is knotted twice as a symbol of making a binding commitment to the creed. ▲

Gurdwara Punja Sahib, Hasan Abdal. Sikh pilgrims swimming in the sacred pond of Punja Sahib Gurdwara. The pond is said to be something ▶
of a miracle, when Guru Nanak put aside a big rock and a pure fountain of water sprang up and began to flow endlessly.

▲ **Katasraj Temples.** The Katasraj Lake located in the Chakwal district of Punjab province is considered to be the second most holy place in Punjab for Hindus after Jawala Mukhi. The water in the lake is said to be the tears of Lord Shiva, mourning the death of his wife. The temple complex built around the lake houses seven temples or sanctuaries dating back at least 1500 years. They were built as a homage to the Hindu deities. When Partition took place all the Hindus living in the area migrated to East India. But relations between Muslims and Hindus in the area was so good, that the local Muslims accompanied their Hindu neighbours on the first stage of their journey to the next town. From there, the Hindus then travelled further and migrated. The magnificent glory of the temples and the vivid pond remained for many centuries until more recently, when the water level deteriorated rapidly as a result of drought and heavy use of ground water for industrial purposes.

◀ **Karachi.** A few miles away from the beachfront where the Parsi community give offerings to the sea on Ava Roj, devotees at Laxmi Mandir are doing the same, except they do this on a daily basis. The offerings they give are the same; coconut, roses and milk.

Kalash Valley. In older times, the Kalash did not bathe in their houses as bathing and washing hair at home was considered impure. With time that changed and ▲ while they now bathe at home, they do go to the river to wash their hair as bathing or washing hair at home is believed to take away blessings.

Ganga Pond, Nagarparkar. A full circle as Hansraj immerses fully into the pond. ►

Acknowledgments

I would like to thank God for giving me the desire to explore and celebrate the diversity of Pakistan. I am thankful for being given the opportunity, patience and resources to travel across the country and interact with the vibrant religious communities of Pakistan, who are an important fabric of our society.

Pakistan is so much more colourful, exciting and complete with all of us put together.

I have learnt more about my own faith, my people and my country after embarking on this journey.

I would like to thank my parents, Salman and Farzana Ansari, for everything they have given me in life – particularly for bringing me up in a tolerant and open-minded household. I would especially like to thank my late grandmother Anver Jehan Ansari, who always encouraged interfaith harmony and often reminisced about the more tolerant days of the past, which made me want to do this book and undertake the journey that was part of the process of making it.

Travelling through the kaleidoscope of faiths and experiencing them firsthand enabled this my seven-year journey to culminate in this book.

I would also like to thank Sayed Gul Kalash, who is an inspiration beyond words and has taken me into the valleys of Kalash and shown me a whole new world. And of course Tulsi Lakhwani for helping me with the initial photography for this book when I did not know where to begin or where to look.

A very special thanks to my incredible uncle (more a friend!) Syed Ahmed Rashid, who was willing to drop what he was doing at the drop of a hat to drive me into the heart of Sindh, enabling me to photograph the vibrant Hindu community that resides there. His vast knowledge of interfaith harmony has played a major part in not just my photography, but in inspiring me to make this book.

Parsis are a very valuable community - not just for Pakistan, but for the subcontinent too. They have played a huge role in the development of Pakistan. I am grateful to Natasha Mavalvalla and her family for making me more aware of the faith, customs and festivities of the Zoroastrian community and for making me a part of all the celebrations. Many thanks to other wonderful friends in the community like Tannaz Minwalla, Minocher Vakharia, Toxy Cowasjee, Homi Ghadially, Berjise Bhada and Veera Rustomji My childhood friend and social media manager Saadan Ahmed Kazi has been a touchstone for my previous and current books.

The accompanying text and sequencing of photographs would not have been possible without the help and advice of my friend Edel Griffith, who has also composed music for my films.

The book cover was a collaboration of many people, including Salman Ansari, Betzabé Hernández Miguel, Imtiaz Hussain and Edel Griffith who all advised and helped me bring the wood to this form.

I cannot fully express my gratefulness to my benefactors: Farrukh Ansari, Salma Ansari, Afia Salam, Sajid Dadabhoy, Umayr Masud, Dr. Asma Ibrahim, Jasmine Michael, Hassan Ali, Mohammad Faisal Khalil, Sindhoo Nawaz, Shahbaz Akbar Chaudhry, Dr. Sono Khangarani, Sanjay Perwani, Amanpreet Singh, Kristina YN, Shahida Saleem, Aurangzeb Bhatti, Aisha Talha Farooqui, Rasheed Noorani, Shehnaz Ismail, the textile design department of Indus Valley School of Art & Architecture, Irum Azeem Farooque, Abdul Sattar Edhi, Rahul Maheshwari, Noreen Haider, Yumna Jawed, Imran Khan, Vijay Maharaj, Byram D. Avari, Rupa James Haroon, Ammar Khan, Nadia Fazal Jamil, Komal Rizvi, Zafar Iqbal, Homi Ghadially, Sabeen Iftikhar, Ushna Moghal, Benazir Shah, Maninder Singh, Adil Siddiq Awan, Ghulam Jilani Shah, Eileen Umar Khitab, Mubashir Mehboob, Asher Mehboob, Leo Joseph Lamuel, Yasir Nisar, Michelle Chaudhry, Syed Sadiq Rashid, Rupa James Haroon, Saarang Mathrani, Amar Guriro, Fatima Wajeeha, Tariq Javed, Ramzan Malik and Khawar Hussain.

All of these people have played the most vital role in mentoring, helping, and educating me about the different faiths in Pakistan and sensitizing me to the beautiful complexity of how we are all so different yet so similar. They helped me in many ways, and sometimes made logistic arrangements for me to photograph certain locations and people. Not to forget my family, friends, strangers and many a name that I may have missed, who have been there for me.

Kiran Aman of Markings has been the persistent driving force of this book, and deserves a huge thanks for her support.

This is not my work alone, but of all of you who have been with me throughout this life-changing journey.